Book
2

Reading for Comprehension
READINESS

Written by Arlene Capriola and Rigmor Swensen
Illustrated by Darcy Bell-Myers and Murray Callahan

ISBN 978-0-8454-3856-5

Copyright © 2007 The Continental Press, Inc.

Continental Press

Can a rabbit be a pet?

A rabbit can be a good pet.
You can get one at a pet shop.

A pet rabbit can live in a house.
It will need a cage with a box.
It will need a dish for food.
It will need a dish for water, too.

A pet rabbit must have room to run.
It can run in a pen outside.
The rabbit is safe in a pen.

  Reading for Comprehension Readiness

Circle the letter for the right answer.

1. This story is about a good _____.

    a name   b pet   c child

2. You can get a rabbit at a _____.

    a zoo   b picnic   c shop

3. A good place for a rabbit to run
   is a _____.

    a house   b cage   c pen

4. You can tell that the rabbit sleeps
   in the _____.

    a box   b car   c tree

Write a word to finish the sentence.

A rabbit needs food and _____.

What kind of bug can sing?

The cricket is a bug.
It is one inch long.
It has six thin legs.

Some crickets live on the ground.
A tree cricket lives in a tree.
Its green color helps it hide.

The male cricket rubs his wings.
That is how he sings.
We can hear his song in summer.

Reading for Comprehension Readiness

Circle the letter for the right answer.

1. This story is about a _____.

   a chicken   b cricket   c rabbit

2. A cricket has six _____.

   a eyes   b wings   c legs

3. The cricket rubs his wings to _____.

   a eat   b sing   c jump

4. A _____ is the best place for a
   cricket to hide.

   a leaf   b root   c house

Write a word to finish the sentence.

_____

_ _

We can hear crickets _____.

What did Walt Disney do?

Walt Disney loved to draw.
He made pictures of a mouse.
He put pants on the mouse.
He made the mouse talk and move.
He gave him a name, Mickey Mouse.
Kids loved Mickey.

Walt made movies with Mickey.
Mickey was on TV, too.
Walt made pictures of other animals.
But Mickey Mouse was the first.

Reading for Comprehension Readiness

Circle the letter for the right answer.

1. This story is about a man who loved to _____.

   a sing   b draw   c sleep

2. Walt Disney made pictures of a _____.

   a mouse   b cat   c rabbit

3. Mickey seemed like a real person because he could _____.

   a draw   b talk   c read

4. You can tell from the story that Mickey did NOT _____.

   a have big ears   b move and talk

                    c look like a real mouse

Write a word to finish the sentence.

_____

- - - - - - - - - - - - -

Mickey Mouse could _____.

Why does a bat have big ears?

Bats live in dark places.
They can not see well in the dark.
But most bats have big ears.
The ears help the bat fly.

The bat makes a sound.
The sound hits the wall.
An echo comes back.
Then the bat can tell where it is.
It can fly in the dark.
And it will not bump into things.

Reading for Comprehension Readiness

Circle the letter for the right answer.

1. This story tells how bats _____.

   a fly   b sleep   c eat

2. A bat can not _____ very well.

   a see   b feel   c hear

3. You can tell from the story that an echo is a _____.

   a picture   b feeling   c sound

4. If you see a bat in the day, it is probably _____.

   a hunting   b sleeping   c playing

Write a word to finish the sentence.

_____

Bats can fly in the _____.

What do toads like?

Toads do not like to be hot.
On hot days they go in the water.
Toads do not like to be cold.
On cold days they stay in a warm place.

When it rains, toads look for an old tree.
The tree is damp.
They go in the tree.
They stay inside.
Then the rain stops.
The toads come out to hunt for worms.

  Reading for Comprehension Readiness

Circle the letter for the right answer.

1. This story is MOSTLY about _____.

   a an animal   b a place   c a tree

2. On hot days, the toad likes to _____.

   a hop   b run   c swim

3. In this story the word <u>damp</u> means _____.

   a cold   b wet   c soft

4. You can tell that the toad looks for a warm place in _____.

   a spring   b summer   c winter

Write a word to finish the sentence.

_____

Toads like to eat _____.

Where is Mexico?

Mexico is a country next to the United States.
It is close to California.

It is hot in Mexico most of the time.
Some people put on sombreros.
A sombrero is a big hat.
It keeps the sun away.

Mexico is by the water.
There are two big seas.
People can swim in the seas.
The water helps them get cool.

Reading for Comprehension Readiness

Circle the letter for the right answer.

1. This story is MOSTLY about a _____.

   a hat   b sea   c country

2. There is a lot of _____ in Mexico.

   a snow   b rain   c sun

3. A sombrero helps MOST when it is _____.

   a hot   b windy   c cold

4. You can tell that the sea is _____.

   a wind   b water   c snow

Write a word to finish the sentence.

_____

- -

The sun makes Mexico _____.

What was Dr. King's dream?

Dr. Martin Luther King had a dream.
His dream was for all of us.
He wanted us to love each other.

Our skin may not be the same.
Our hair may not be the same.
But inside we are all the same.

We must be good to each other.
Then we will all be happy.
That was Dr. King's dream.

  Reading for Comprehension Readiness

Circle the letter for the right answer.

1. This story is about _____.

   a a man   b some kids   c our dreams

2. Dr. King had a _____ for all of us.

   a gift   b school   c dream

3. He wanted us to _____ each other.

   a see   b love   c miss

4. Dr. King's dream was for a _____ world.

   a sad   b happy   c bigger

Write a word to finish the sentence.

_____

We all do not have the same _____.

What animal can live in water?

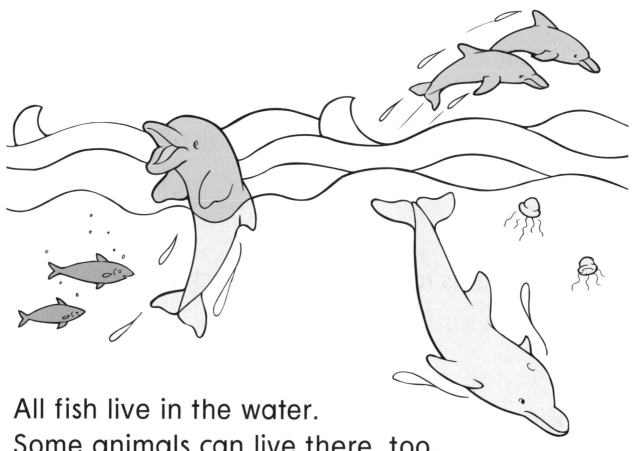

All fish live in the water.
Some animals can live there, too.
One animal dives way down in the water.
But it is not a fish.
So it must come up to get air.

This animal is a dolphin.
It likes to swim.
It looks for fish to eat.
It likes to play, too.
The dolphin can jump out of the water.

  Reading for Comprehension Readiness

Circle the letter for the right answer.

1. This story is about _____ that lives in the water.

   a an animal   b a fish   c a turtle

2. It likes to _____.

   a fly   b play   c think

3. It can jump _____.

   a on the sand   b on ships

   c out of the water

4. You can tell that it _____.

   a has big wings   b is very small

   c needs air to live

Write a word to finish the sentence.

_____

- -

Dolphins like to eat _____.

What is a seed?

A plant has seeds.
But all seeds are not the same.
A peach has one big seed.
An apple has many little seeds.

There is a tiny plant inside the seed.
You can plant the seed in dirt.
You must give it water.
It will need sun, too.

It will grow into a plant.
It will look just like the mother plant.
And it will have seeds, too!

  Reading for Comprehension Readiness

Circle the letter for the right answer.

1. This story tells MOSTLY about the

   _____.

   a apple   b peach   c seed

2. An apple has _____ seeds.

   a big   b many   c ten

3. Plants must have _____ to grow.

   a flowers   b water   c fire

4. Every seed can grow to be a _____.

   a plant   b apple   c tree

Write a word to finish the sentence.

_____

A peach has one _____.

Who is Uncle Sam?

Uncle Sam is not a real man.
You may see him in pictures.
Uncle **S**am stands for the **U.S.**
The **U.S.** is the **U**nited **S**tates.
So, Uncle Sam stands for our country.

Uncle Sam is tall and thin.
His coat and pants are red, white, and blue.
He has a big hat with stars.
You may see him in a parade, too.
If you do, wave to him!

Reading for Comprehension Readiness

Circle the letter for the right answer.

1. This story tells about a man in a _____.

   a car   b book   c picture

2. The U.S. is a _____.

   a country   b family   c city

3. The name <u>Uncle Sam</u> stands for _____.

   a a book   b the U.S.   c a picture

4. Uncle Sam's clothes are the colors of _____.

   a a map   b our flag   c your school

Write a word to finish the sentence.

_____

On Uncle Sam's hat there are _____.

Go To Fun Page 38

What is the moon like?

The moon is far away from Earth.
It has no air.
It has a lot of dust.
Nothing lives there.

The moon is big and round.
It has large holes and many rocks.
At night, the sun lights up the moon.

Some men have been on the moon.
They went in space ships.
Then they came back to Earth.
They told us what the moon is like.

Circle the letter for the right answer.

1. This story is about the _____.

    a sun   b Earth   c moon

2. The moon does NOT have _____.

    a air   b holes   c dust

3. The moon gets _____ from the sun.

    a rain   b light   c rocks

4. _____ can live on the moon.

    a Animals   b Plants   c Nothing

Write a word to finish the sentence.

_____

We live on _____.

Why does the butterfly like flowers?

A butterfly can have many colors.
It can be yellow and black.
It can be blue and red, too.

A butterfly flaps its big wings.
It goes from flower to flower.
It helps the flower make seeds.
Then more flowers can grow.

The butterfly gets nectar from the flowers.
It flies to the flower it likes best.
Then it stays very still.
It can sit there a long time.

Circle the letter for the right answer.

1. This story is about a kind of _____.

   a bug   b bird   c pet

2. The butterfly can have lots of _____.

   a legs   b teeth   c colors

3. In this story, <u>nectar</u> is the _____ the butterfly likes.

   a flower   b food   c home

4. You can tell that the flower and the butterfly _____ each other.

   a need   b hold   c find

Write a word to finish the sentence.

_____

_ _ _ _ _ _ _ _ _ _ _ _ _ _ _ _ _ _ _ _

A butterfly can sit very _____.

How did the Pilgrims come to America?

Long ago, the Pilgrims came to America.
They set out in a big ship.
It was a hard trip.
But the Pilgrims wanted a new life.

The trip was long.
Big waves rocked the ship.
The Pilgrims lost their way.
Then they saw a place to land.

The Pilgrims saw trees to make houses.
There was water to drink.
There were plants to eat.
The Pilgrims made a new home in America.

Reading for Comprehension Readiness

Circle the letter for the right answer.

1. This story is MOSTLY about _____.

   a a ship   b some people   c big waves

2. The Pilgrims wanted to have a _____.

   a new home   b good ship   c hard trip

3. Logs from trees can make good _____.

   a farms   b food   c houses

4. You can tell that the Pilgrims were _____ on the ship at sea.

   a lost   b safe   c sick

Write a word to finish the sentence.

_____

The Pilgrims stayed in _____.

Can trees help the Earth?

It is fun to plant a tree.
You can watch it grow.
Trees give us shade from the sun.
Birds find a safe home there.

Trees help the Earth, too.
Some gas is bad for the Earth.
It makes the Earth warmer and warmer.
Trees take in this gas.
They use it.
Then they give out the gas we need.

Kids can help the Earth.
Just plant a tree.

  Reading for Comprehension Readiness

Circle the letter for the right answer.

1. This story tells how _____ helps the Earth.

   a the sun   **b** gas   **c** a tree

2. _____ like to live in trees.

   a Kids   **b** Birds   **c** Cats

3. Some gas makes the Earth too _____.

   a warm   **b** clean   **c** cold

4. You can tell that _____ gas is good for the Earth.

   a no   **b** some   **c** all

Write a word to finish the sentence.

_____

You can _____ a tree to help the Earth.

How did Helen Keller talk?

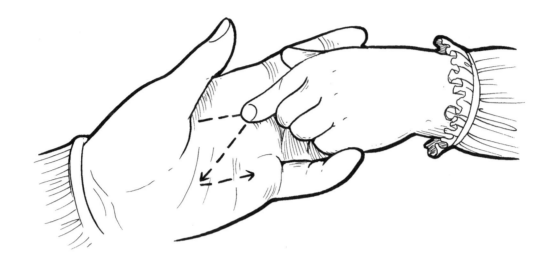

Helen Keller liked to pet the cow.
But she could not see the cow.
She could not hear it "moo."

When Helen was a baby she got sick.
After that she could not see or hear.
So, she could not talk.
That made her mad.
She hit people and kicked and bit them.

Then Anne came to teach Helen.
Anne made words with her fingers.
Soon Helen could use her hands to make words.
Now she had a way to talk.

Circle the letter for the right answer.

1. This story is about a _____.

   a cow   b girl   c baby

2. Helen was _____ when she was a baby.

   a bad   b big   c sick

3. She could NOT _____ the cow.

   a feel   b see   c smell

4. Helen hit and bit people because she could NOT _____.

   a talk   b sleep   c walk

Write a word to finish the sentence.

_____

Helen made words with her _____.

How did people use pictures for words?

The first Americans did not write words.
They used pictures.
A picture was like a word.

The first Americans had to hunt for meat.
The pictures tell about this.
They tell about the sun and the rain, too.

Their pictures were many colors.
They were red and yellow.
They were green and blue, too.
The colors came from grass and plants.

Look at the pictures.
Can you make a story with them?

Reading for Comprehension Readiness

Circle the letter for the right answer.

I. This story is MOSTLY about _____.

    a people   b plants   c words

2. The first Americans used _____ to tell a story.

    a pens   b colors   c books

3. The first Americans needed to _____ for food.

    a hunt   b write   c dig

4. We can tell about long ago from their _____.

    a trees   b animals   c pictures

Write a word to finish the sentence.

_____

The first Americans made colors from _____.

CAN A RABBIT BE A PET?

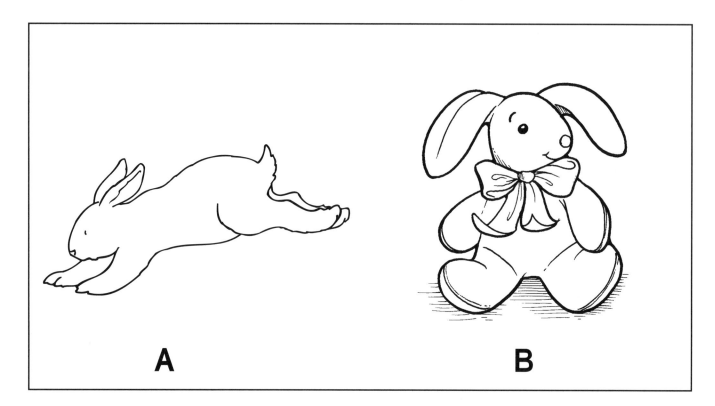

A

B

Which rabbit?

⊙ Write **A** or **B** on the line to answer each question.

1. Which rabbit will get bigger? _____

2. Which rabbit has fur? _____

3. Which rabbit can not hop? _____

⊙ Color the pictures.

  Skills: Reality vs. Fantasy and Following Directions

WHAT DID WALT DISNEY DO?

Walt Disney made funny pictures.
Sometimes he used ▽ △ □ ○ to start.

⊙ Make a funny picture in the box.
Use the picture to help you.
Or make up your own.

⊙ Color your funny picture.

Fun Page

WHAT DO TOADS LIKE?

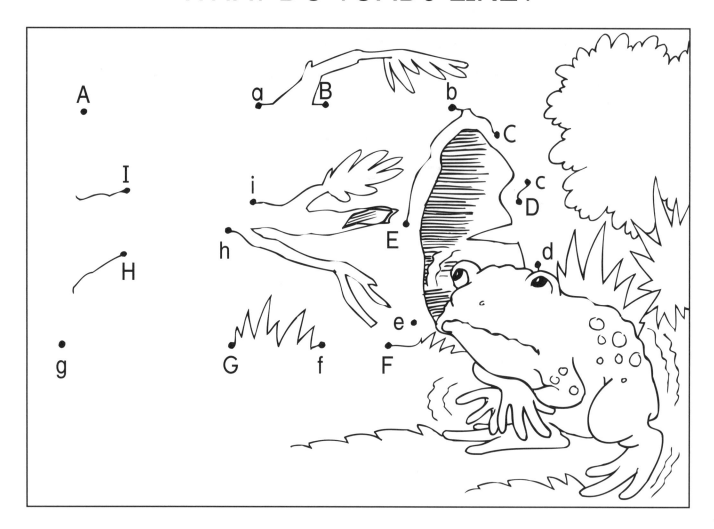

It is cold.
Help this animal find a warm place.

⊙ Match the letters.

⊙ Go from A to a.
Then do the other letters.

⊙ Color the picture.

 Skills: Letter Recognition and Noting Similarities © The Continental Press, Inc. Do not duplicate.

Fun Page

WHAT WAS DR. KING'S DREAM?

We all do not look the same.

⊙ Make our skin: <u>brown</u> and <u>pink</u> and <u>yellow</u>.

⊙ Make our hair: <u>black</u> and <u>red</u> and <u>brown</u>.

We must love each other.

⊙ Put a ♡ on all of us.

WHO IS UNCLE SAM?

⊙ Help Uncle Sam lead the parade.
Do not cross the lines.

⊙ Color the street the parade can go on.

⊙ Make it red or blue.

WHY DOES THE BUTTERFLY LIKE FLOWERS?

Color by number.

⊙ Color the butterfly.

1 — Orange	3 — Brown
2 — Yellow	4 — Purple

Skills: Fine Motor and Following Directions

Fun Page

CAN TREES HELP THE EARTH?

⊙ Put 1, 2, or 3 in the box to show the order.

First, you plant a tree.

Then, it grows.

Last, birds make nests in the tree.

⊙ Color the pictures.

  Skills: Sequencing and Following Directions